MW00899360

Wildlife Rescue and Rehabilitation Worker

Ruth Bjorklund

Cavendish
Square

New York

Published in 2014 by Cavendish Square Publishing, LLC
303 Park Avenue South, Suite 1247, New York, NY 10010

Library of Congress Cataloging-in-Publication Data
Bjorklund, Ruth.
Wildlife rescue and rehabilitation worker / by Ruth Bjorklund.
p. cm. — (Careers with animals)
Includes index.
ISBN 978-1-62712-470-6 (hardcover) ISBN 978-1-62712-471-3 (paperback) ISBN 978-1-62712-472-0 (ebook)
1. Wildlife rescue — Juvenile literature. 2. Animal specialists — Vocational guidance — United States — Juvenile literature. I. Bjorklund, Ruth. II. Title.
QL83.2 B56 2014
639.9—dc23

Editorial Director: Dean Miller
Senior Editor: Peter Mavrikis
Copy Editor: Fran Hatton
Art Director: Jeffrey Talbot
Designer: Amy Greenan
Photo Researcher: Julie Alissi, J8 Media
Production Manager: Jennifer Ryder-Talbot
Production Editor: Andrew Coddington

Printed in the United States of America

CONTENTS

ONE

Making the Connection

Some people know at a young age that they love animals and want to work with them and care for them throughout their lives. But some people, like wildlife rehabilitator Mike Pratt, discover their passion by surprise. Mike was a part-time emergency medical technician (EMT) and worked for a small-town fire department. He was attending college taking general education classes. He also volunteered at a local wild animal shelter. One night, Mike was the last one to leave the shelter. He turned off the lights and reached for the door. After a long day of school, work, and volunteering, he was tired and eager to go home. But just as he stepped outside, the telephone rang. An accident had happened on the highway coming into town. The driver was not seriously hurt, but the car had hit a pregnant deer, forcing her fawn to be born prematurely. Mike got into his car and drove to the scene.

The mother deer was dead. Police cars were blinking their lights as traffic snaked slowly around the accident site. A police officer brought Mike over to his squad car, where in the back seat was a tiny fawn curled up in a blanket. The officer had turned the heater on high trying to keep the helpless newborn alive. Mike took the fawn back to the shelter. He gave her fluids,

(Opposite) A wildlife rehabilitation worker feeds an orphaned fawn.

This orphaned baby deer has little chance of survival without the help of a wildlife rehabilitator. (Opposite) A mural showing ancient Egyptian farmers working with their oxen-drawn plows.

kept her warm, and sat by her side all night. The baby fawn survived the night. In the following months, with the dedicated attention of the shelter's wildlife rehabilitators, the fawn grew healthy and strong. Eventually the fawn was released back into the forest where she belonged. Saving that baby deer taught Mike all he needed to know about what his future would be. "That first night was when I knew. That tiny deer and her struggle to live took me in. I knew then I was always going to help the wild stay wild."

Mike took a look at the classes he had been taking in college and realized he needed to focus his studies on what would be his life's passion. He completed the classes required to earn a **bachelor of science** in wildlife biology. Although a four-year degree in wildlife biology is not required, it provides an excellent background. A college degree isn't necessary to become licensed as a wildlife rehabilitator. Wildlife rehabilitation is a very competitive field, however, and a bachelor's degree in a biology-related field of study is a definite advantage.

Wildlife rescue and rehabilitation requires a wide variety of skills and talents. Generally wildlife rescue centers are small **nonprofit** operations and workers are often expected to perform most any task when the need arises. Wildlife rehabilitators come to their careers in wildlife rehabilitation from several different directions. Some have studied and /or worked as educators, nurses, veterinarians, and veterinary technicians. Some have been wetlands biologists, ecologists, foresters, landscapers, park rangers, fund-raisers, and

public administrators. What unites any and all wildlife rescue and rehabilitation workers is a deep respect for wild animals and their habitat. "It is a privilege to be so near a wild animal," one rescue worker said about her job.

Humans and Animals

Since early times, humans have captured and tamed, or **domesticated**, animals to work for them for mutual survival. They trained dogs for protection and to help them hunt for food. They kept cats to rid their homes of vermin. As human civilization progressed, humans trained animals for transportation and to pull plows and haul heavy belongings. For this, they captured oxen, wild horses, elephants, camels, and llamas. Noblemen in

(Top) A wildlife rescue worker holds a fox cub.
(Left) These great horned owls were brought to the St. Francis Wildlife Association Rehabilitation Center in Florida for treatment of their injuries. Once completely healed, they will be released back into the wild.
(Bottom) A wildlife rescue worker feeds a river otter.

Is a Career as a Wildlife Rescue and Rehabilitation Worker Right for You?

If you are interested in being a wildlife rescue and rehabilitation worker, start with a look at this checklist to see if you might be a good fit for the job.

Do you like caring for animals?

Do you like nature and being outdoors?

Are you interested in health care?

Are you flexible, and can you handle the unexpected?

Are you patient?

Are you interested in science and natural history?

Do you enjoy sharing what you know with others?

To avoid frightening this baby rabbit, a rehabilitation worker wears gloves to handle it.

Europe were often falconers. They trained birds of prey to help them hunt foxes, pheasants, and rabbits. In parts of Asia, fishers used cormorants to catch their fish. After a time, domesticated animals no longer knew how to fend for themselves in the wild and came to rely on humans for their survival.

Most animals, however, were never domesticated. Animals in the wild do not need the help of humans to survive until the lives of humans and wild animals collide. Every day, around the world, human development and activity intrudes on the habitats of wild animals. When a wild animal becomes the victim in an encounter with humans, it is the role of a wildlife rehabilitation worker to help the animal recover and return to the wild.

Ancient Greeks domesticated dogs and cats as pets as shown in this carving.

(Opposite) A rock drawing from the 1st century depicts a hunter on horseback.

TWO

Choosing Your Path

A wildlife rehabilitator rescues wild animals that are sick, injured, or orphaned. He or she attempts to save the animal and return it to its natural place in the wild. Many wildlife rehabilitators have an educational background in animal health or behavior. Others have degrees in ecology, biology, or zoology. There is not at this time a college or university in the United States that offers a degree specifically in wildlife rehabilitation. However there are many degrees that can lead to a successful career in wildlife rehabilitation.

Starting Early

Wildlife rehabilitation is a worthwhile and rewarding field. Working with animals is the dream of many. But to people seriously considering a career working with wildlife, gaining practical knowledge is important. Not every day in the life of a wildlife rehabilitator is exciting. Workers spend time doing regular daily tasks and additional duties that help make a shelter run smoothly. So, it is a good idea to get a feel for the job at an early age. If a career saving wildlife is your goal, there are many actions you can take to give yourself a good head start.

(Opposite) Rescue workers in the field quickly put a splint on the broken leg of this hedgehog.

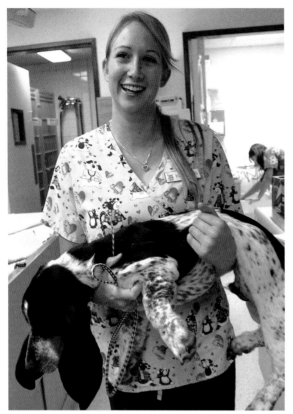

A young woman volunteers at a local animal shelter.

Look Around

Explore all you can about animals and their behavior. Spend time reading books and watching programs about wild animals. Check out educational wildlife sites on the Internet. Most zoos have excellent websites. Learn about the habits of wildlife near where you live. You may live near deer, coyotes, eagles, herons, and foxes or songbirds, geese, squirrels, and raccoons. Try to recognize birdsongs and birdcalls and remember the names of the animals you see. Go for walks or hikes in natural settings where you can look for signs of wild animals and their nests, droppings, sounds, trails, and watering spots.

Camps, Clubs, and Volunteering

It is important to take advantage of any opportunity you can to get hands-on experience with animals. If there is a 4-H program, a school environmental club, or Future Farmers of America group in your area, consider joining.

There are a variety of volunteer opportunities available to young people interested in working with animals. Good sources for volunteer opportunities include contacting a nearby wildlife shelter, the humane society, a local zoo, the parks department, or state ecology or wildlife departments. There is at least one National Wildlife Refuge in every state. Visit their website to find one near you for programs, events, and volunteer activities. Some openings require a person to be at least 16 years of age, so it is important to call first and get the facts.

Older students may want to investigate summer volunteer positions with the Youth **Conservation** Corps of the U.S. Fish and Wildlife Service, the Bureau of Land Management, the National Park Service, state environmental agencies or local branches of nonprofit organizations such as the Sierra Club, Nature Conservancy, Audubon Society, or the Society

Campers at 4-H camp learn to care for animals.

for the Prevention of Cruelty to Animals (SPCA). While many of these volunteer positions may not include working directly with wild animals, they do provide experience in becoming familiar with wild animal habitats.

Summer camps and day camps are another way to gain valuable experience working with animals. Look online or contact veterinary schools and wildlife organizations for information on where to attend animal science camps or "Jr. Vet" camps. These programs allow campers to observe wildlife up close and learn about their native habitats. Campers learn to identify the symptoms of sick animals and help with medical exams. They also learn rehabilitation techniques and how to properly handle and feed the animals. Campers participate in typical day-to-day chores such as cleaning and building animal **enclosures**.

School

Wildlife rehabilitators and rescue workers encourage people who want to work with wild animals to take life science classes in middle school and high school. These foundation subjects include anatomy, biology, **physiology**, zoology, and biochemistry. Also important are physical sciences, such as chemistry, physics, and mathematics. Licensed rehabilitators also emphasize taking **natural history** courses in order to observe how animals behave in their natural environment.

Staying the Course

The National Wildlife Rehabilitator's Association (NWRA) recommends a college degree in ecology or biology. Wildlife conservation and animal medicine courses also provide an excellent background to become a licensed wildlife rehabilitator. The NWRA recommends classes in **ornithology** (study of birds), mammalogy (study of mammals), animal behavior, ecology, animal physiology (the study of how organs and systems in the body function), natural history, and other wildlife and environmental subjects. Furthermore, the NWRA emphasizes the need to include a variety of other subjects, especially English and humanities classes. Wildlife workers interpret technical and medical information to the general public, so writing and public speaking skills are important qualifications.

Knowing what an animal does to survive in its environment is a critical part of the job of wildlife rehabilitator. One rehabilitator, for example, wrote about a boy and his family who had found an orphaned baby dove. The family called the wildlife shelter, but there wasn't a way to transport the baby chick that day. The rehabilitator explained that a baby dove feeds by diving its head inside its mother's mouth to get food she has placed there. So the boy found a plastic toy shark with a big flexible mouth and he put food inside. The baby dove responded by ducking its head in the toy's mouth to eat. When the family brought the baby dove to the shelter a few days later, rescue workers told the boy he had saved its life.

This student has an internship in a genetics laboratory.

Typical requirements for an animal-related bachelor of science degree:

Biology

Microbiology

Physics

Zoology

Botany

Biochemistry

Organic and Inorganic Chemistry

Anatomy

Animal Physiology

Ornithology

Mammalogy

Anthropology

Genetics

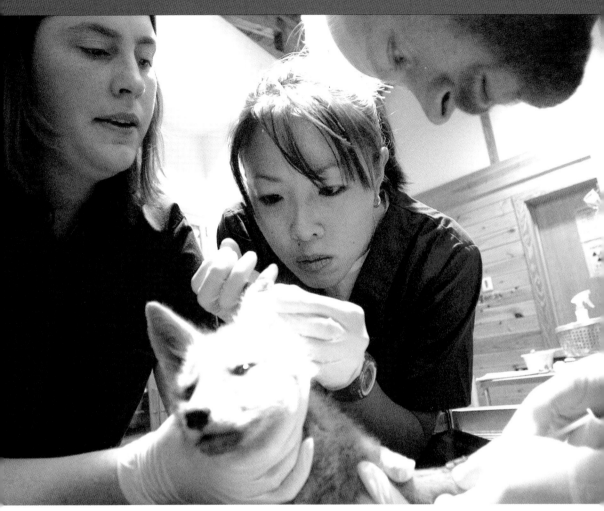

A student in a veterinarian technician program is helping to treat an injured fox.

Although there is no formal degree in wildlife rehabilitation, many colleges and universities offer classes in animal science, wildlife management, field techniques, animal restraint, wildlife care, and pre-veterinary medicine. There are more than sixty colleges that offer veterinary technology or animal health classes. Some schools are located near wildlife rehabilitation centers and offer college credit while working as an intern. There are twenty-eight universities around the country that offer a graduate degree in veterinary medicine. Many of these schools have **undergraduate** classes in wildlife care and wildlife medicine.

19

Veterinary Technician

There are more than 100 veterinary technician schools that offer an **associate of science** degree and are accredited by the American Veterinary Medical Association (AVMA). Fifteen offer a four-year bachelor of science as well. Veterinary technicians do not go through the extensive program that a doctor of veterinary medicine does, but they are an important asset to animal care. Many licensed wildlife rehabilitators have a veterinary technician background. Their clinic skills are in high demand.

Veterinary technicians learn to run medical tests, take X-rays, and administer medicine while under the supervision of a veterinarian. Some larger wildlife rehabilitation centers have their own clinic facilities where rehabilitators perform the tasks of a veterinary technician. If you are considering earning an associate degree in veterinary technology and want to pursue working as a wildlife rehabilitator, be sure to add wildlife biology, ecology, and natural history to your studies. A veterinary technician must pass the Veterinary Technician National Exam to become licensed. The exam contains 200 questions. Further regulations and requirements for licensing vary by state.

Applying for School

If you plan to attend a four-year college or university, there are countless possibilities for finding a good bachelor of science program. Of course financial considerations and the school's location are very important. But once you have an idea of what you can pay and where you are able to live, then the task of choosing a school begins. To determine what's best for you, consider the size and depth of the biology and ecology departments. Do they offer courses in wildlife biology, wildlife ecology, animal behavior, or wildlife conservation? Find out if there is a veterinary school affiliated

Birds are the most common animals found in rehabilitation centers. Here, a brown pelican is being treated for a broken wing.

with the institution. Are there undergraduate courses in animal health and natural history? Are there student associations such as a student chapter of the Wildlife Society or a Student Conservation Association? Investigate if there are any wildlife rehabilitation centers, zoos, or wildlife refuges located nearby. People looking for a veterinary technician program should prepare by contacting schools and asking questions. Be sure, first of all, that it is accredited by the AVMA. Other questions include:

- How many students complete the program in a reasonable time period?
- What percentage of students who graduate from the school pass the National Veterinary Technician Exam?
- Is there a "Vet Tech" student association?
- How many graduates are typically employed within three to four months of graduation?
- Cost? Is financial aid available?

Internships

An internship is one of the best preparations for a career in wildlife rescue and rehabilitation. Interns can gain valuable hands-on experience working in wildlife habitats and observing wildlife activity. Internships are entry-level jobs where you receive practical training. Many internships are unpaid positions, but others provide a small salary. Numerous high school, university, and college science departments offer summer science and biology internship

There are many interesting opportunities for interning with federal government agencies.

Contact them early for summer internship applications. Most positions are filled by January or February. Call or write:

- National Wildlife Refuge System (NWR)
  www.fws.gov/refuges
- National Park Service (NPS)
  www.nps.gov/aboutus/jobsforstudents.htm
- U.S. Department of Fish and Wildlife (USFW)
  www.fws.gov/jobs/
- Student Conservation Association
  www.thesca.org
- U.S. Environmental Protection Agency (EPA)
  www.epa.gov/careers/internships/
- National Oceanic and Atmospheric Administration (NOAA)
  www.education.noaa.gov/Special_Topics/
- Bureau of Land Management (BLM) Student
  Temporary Employment Program
  www.blm.gov
- Youth at U.S. Geological Survey (USGS)
  www.usgs.gov/ohr/students/
- Migratory Bird Protection Corps
  www.fws.gov/migratorybirds

In the future, as a wildlife rehabilitator, you will often work closely with these state and federal agencies.

A wildlife biology student has a summer job doing field work for the U.S. Fish and Wildlife Department.

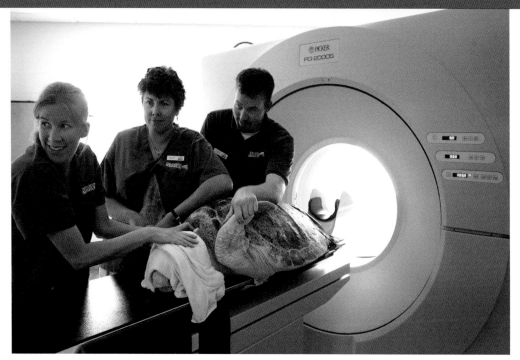

Rehabilitation workers need a special license to work with endangered species, such as this loggerhead turtle.

programs. You can also contact local zoos, humane societies, parks, nature centers, outdoor recreation centers, nature preserves, and government agencies. Several of the agencies that have internship programs offer scholarships for college or technical school, so it is an advantage to be well known to the agency and its employees.

Becoming Licensed

Wildlife rehabilitators hold permits or licenses from both the state and federal governments, depending on the animals they work with. There may also be a permit or license required by local cities or counties. Some wildlife rehabilitation centers hold an organizational license, and you may not need to own one privately. However, there are many responsibilities in a rehabilitation center and your employers may need you to be licensed. Requirements differ from state to state. Contact your state's wildlife management, environment, ecology, or conservation departments, or a regional office of the U.S. Fish and Wildlife Service Migratory Bird Permit Section for permit information. To obtain a federal permit, contact the U.S. Fish and Wildlife Service for requirements, an information packet, and an application. The U.S. Fish and Wildlife Service oversees migratory birds and nationally threatened and **endangered species**. States are responsible for non-migratory birds, mammals, reptiles and amphibians, and any native threatened species.

Before you can receive your permit, you must meet several requirements including special training, internship programs or hands-on volunteering experience, and an oral or written exam. The permit information packet will tell you what you need to do to qualify. After receiving a permit, wildlife rehabilitators take classes on wildlife medicine, attend conferences, and participate in continuing education workshops. They also read books and articles on the latest developments and network with other people associated with wildlife rescue and rehabilitation. The National Wildlife Rehabilitation Association and the International Wildlife Rehabilitators Council publish many of the most essential books, articles, and reports. Becoming a wildlife rescue and rehabilitation worker requires years of patience and focus, but rehabilitators say their rewards are worth all the hard work.

THREE

Day to Day

There are several interesting types of jobs working with wildlife, but none are more hands-on than the job of a wildlife rescue and rehabilitation worker. Wildlife rescue workers go into the field and attend to wild animals. They assess the extent of the harm and decide whether or not the animal needs human intervention to survive. If they do, the workers transport the animals to a rehabilitation facility where rehabilitators will provide 24-hour a day care.

Wildlife Rescue Workers

Wildlife rescue workers are animal **first responders**, much like firefighters, EMTs, or police officers. Wildlife rescue workers respond to emergency calls and perform animal **triage**. A wildlife rescue worker must handle the animal with caution and address its problems quickly before delivering the animal to a rehabilitator. If the distressed animal is large, such as a raccoon, opossum, eagle, heron, deer, fox, wolf, or coyote, it will be caught in a safe trap or sedated. In this case, an experienced wildlife rehabilitator should be present.

(Opposite) Baby seals are often hunted illegally for their pelts. Here rescue workers are trying to calm the animal before transferring it to a marine mammal rescue center.

Wildlife rescue workers and rehabilitators are responsible for stabilizing the animal before bringing it to the rehabilitation center. The most serious concern is the likelihood the animal is in shock. Shock is a reduction in blood flow and loss of fluids and body heat caused by injury, sickness, or severe trauma. Stress also contributes to shock. The animal is stressed not only from pain, but from the sounds, sights, and smells of human activity. Out of fear and an instinct for survival, animals will bite or lash out while being handled. If the animal is bleeding, rescue workers apply pressure and sometimes medication. If the animal has a broken bone and is trying to use its leg or wing, the rescue worker will make a temporary splint. After an initial assessment, they wrap the animal, keep it warm, if necessary give it fluids, and place it in a covered box or safe trap to transport to the rehabilitation center or clinic. The key to the transportation process is keeping things quiet, dark, and warm.

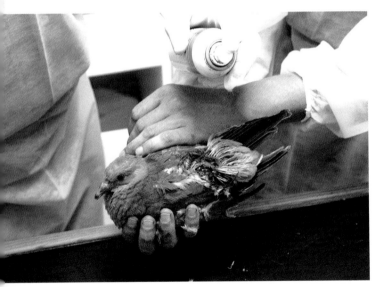

When animals are severely injured, immediate treatment is administered in the field.

Animal Triage

Animal triage is a scientific method used to determine the extent of an animal's illness or injury. Wildlife rehabilitators perform animal triage at rehabilitation centers as well as in the field. They must think quickly and make the

Rescuing frightened and dangerous animals is risky, and rescue workers must have professional expertise.

When off-shore oil drills, oil pipelines, and oil tankers malfunction, water birds, ducks, and marine animals suffer the consequences.

best use of whatever resources are at hand. In triage, rehabilitators make decisions about the animal's likely survival. They examine animals using a series of medical tests that measure important things such as heart rate, pulse, breathing, and **neurological** status. They look for excessive bleeding, pain, and muscle and skeletal injuries. In order for the animal to receive the best possible care, rehabilitators must categorize the animal's condition. There are four categories—minor, immediate, urgent, and **euthanize**. Unlike human triage or domesticated animal triage, wildlife triage results in the healthiest animals given the best treatment. In wildlife rehabilitation, the mission is to return a wild animal back to its native habitat as a fully functioning member of its group. If the animal is too disabled to return to the wild, it will either starve or be eaten. Given that outcome, it is more humane to euthanize a severely injured wild animal. An animal that is likely to survive whether or not it receives treatment usually goes back to its territory, den, or nest. Otherwise, it is taken in for an observation period before being released. Licensing rules require that in nearly all cases, rehabilitators must release wild animals in six months or less, or else euthanize the animals.

It takes more than 45 minutes to clean a bird injured in an oil spill.

Most rehabilitation facilities care for birds, **waterfowl**, raptors, and small mammals. Some are licensed for larger mammals, such as wolves, foxes, wild cats, and bears. Birds, ducks, rabbits, raccoons, and squirrels are the most common casualties of human/ wildlife encounters. Sometimes the situation is slight, such as a bird becoming stunned by flying into a window. Other times, emergencies can be dire, such as when birds, shorebirds, and waterfowl are affected by toxic waste and oil spills. One of the most important responsibilities of a rehabilitator is to prepare for these events. Each state must have an oil spill plan in place to treat affected wildlife. States generally rely on wildlife rehabilitators to perform the work. Rehabilitators must have a special certification from the government to operate clean-up programs.

Wildlife Educators

According to federal and state laws, licensed wildlife rehabilitators must rehabilitate wild animals and release them back into the wild within 180 days. Animals unable to survive in the wild, whether due to the severity of their injury or an over-dependency on humans, must be euthanized. The only exception is for "education animals." Education animals are unable to survive in the wild, but there are laws that allow them to remain in **captivity** if they are used in presentations to the public. Generally, education animals are birds of prey, such as bald eagles, ospreys, or great horned owls. Lisa Horn explains that education animals cannot be treated as pets. "It is important to let the animals keep their dignity by leaving some of the wild in them." She says that an education animal and its rehabilitator/handler are the most persuasive ambassadors for wildlife protection.

In presentations to the public, wildlife rehabilitation educators describe their role and the importance of saving wildlife. A frequent question from people is, "Why spend time and money to save wild animals when there are so many problems in the world?" A rehabilitator's best response is that most injured or orphaned animals are suffering because of human interaction—car accidents, trains, mowers, poisons, oil spills, logging, forest fires, pollution, and more. Lisa Horn says, "Wild animals are a barometer of how your environment is working, if your animals are sick and suffering, then we say you need to be looking at yourselves to fix the problem."

Rehabilitation educators often use raptors in their presentations to the public.

FOUR

Work Environments

Most wildlife rehabilitators work in centers that function for that precise purpose. Basic responsibilities are to prepare food, feed animals, and clean animal enclosures daily. Shona Aitken, the education director at Wolf Hollow Rehabilitation Center in Friday Harbor, Washinton, laughed when she described the main job of a "rehabber" as "feed, clean, prep, repeat." She says that being a wildlife rehabilitator is the opportunity of a lifetime, but it can be at times routine, or even outright unpleasant. "Sometimes we have to do things like rescue an angry opossum that has fallen into a park outhouse. That is NOT glamorous!"

Spring is the busiest time of year for rehabilitation centers, and they usually hire seasonal workers and extra volunteers. It is the so-called baby season, and incidences of young animals being injured or orphaned increase. Babies are placed in **incubators** or small enclosures designed to resemble their natural nest or den. Rehabilitators prepare special food and must hand-feed the babies around the clock. They resist the inclination to cuddle or comfort the baby animal so that it will not become attached or dependent on humans.

Trained rehabilitators rely on their knowledge of natural history and animal behavior to design and build appropriate animal enclosures. "We call them enclosures, not cages," explains Mike Pratt. It is important to construct

Expert rehabilitators are able to assess whether a young animal is orphaned, lost, or just temporarily separated from its mother.

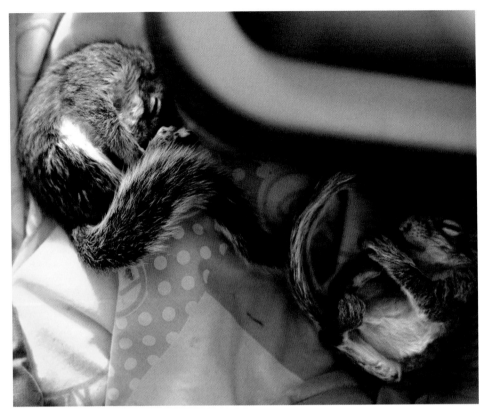

Orphaned Eastern gray squirrels—about a month old—sleep inside an incubator. (Opposite) Eagles, hawks, falcons, and other raptors need to be housed in large enclosures to allow the animals enough room for flight.

enclosures according to species, size, age, and health status. He explains that foxes need to retreat to a den, cougars need big spaces to run in, squirrels chew through thin wire and must have strong enclosures, and bobcats and deer jump high so they need high fences or covers. Waterfowl and shorebirds need nesting areas and filtered pools of clean water. Federal law requires that rehabilitators provide raptors with large enclosures so that eagles and hawks can practice flight before they are released. Animals ready to be released must practice hunting and killing their own food, so rehabilitators raise mice for feed. The education director at Wolf Hollow is reassuring, saying, "Don't worry

about the mice, they live like princesses and princes until their last day!"

Most rehabilitation centers have exam rooms and small clinics. Few have veterinarians on staff full time, so rehabilitators provide most daily medical care. They are responsible for medications, monitoring **vital signs**, dressing wounds, laboratory tests, X-rays, watching for infections or changes in eating habits, and any other signs of distress. Licensed rehabilitators are required to release an animal within 180 days. If an animal is unable to survive on its own by that time, a rehabilitator who is a registered and authorized euthanasia technician then euthanizes it.

Environmental Education Programs and Centers

Many wildlife rehabilitators educate the public about nature conservation and protection. Most rehabilitation centers have an education director who visits schools, parks, public events, and community groups. Rehabilitation educators interpret animal behavior and natural history for the public. They also use "education animals" in their presentations. Other than rehabilitation facilities, wildlife rehabilitation educators also work in natural history museums, government environmental agencies, wilderness centers, animal refuges, parks, and zoos.

Government Agencies and Programs

In 2005, Congress required that each state develop a State Wildlife Action Plan. The plans mapped out ways that local wildlife and the habitats within them could be conserved presently and into the future. Because of these action plans, state agencies such as departments of ecology, fish and wildlife, environmental protection, and parks services employ wildlife rehabilitators to guide them in their efforts toward wildlife conservation. Most government wildlife rehabilitators attend to animals in the field, in their natural habitat. If long-term rehabilitation is needed, the animals are usually turned over to a rehabilitation center. Government wildlife rehabilitators are responsible for managing volunteers and other rehabilitators during disasters that affect wildlife such as forest fires, major storms, and oil spills.

Independent rehabilitators

Traditionally, wildlife rehabilitation was an occupation of independent rehabilitators. Many worked out of their homes. Several decades ago, it was considered almost a hobby. Today however, all rehabilitators need to be trained and licensed. Independent rehabilitators bear much of the burden of the costs involved in caring for distressed wildlife. They must rely predominantly on donations to support their activities. The number of independent rehabilitators is dwindling as a result.

Many independent rehabilitators focus on specific types of animals, such as reptiles, wolves, or birds.

Wildlife Rescue Sanctuaries

Persons permanently caring for sick, injured, orphaned, or abandoned wildlife in **wildlife refuges or sanctuaries** are not technically wildlife rehabilitators. Although they have similar tasks, their mission and licensing differ. Wild animals in refuges or sanctuaries are not rehabilitated so they can be released later. They are treated and cared for in captivity for the rest of their lives. Many of these animals are exotic animals that were once pets, sometimes illegally, such as cougars, leopards, wolves, chimpanzees, and bobcats. Wildlife rescue workers get involved when the animals' owners are unable or unwilling to properly care for them.

This young bobcat is being treated at a wildlife rehabilitation center in Eudora, Mississippi.

Rehabilitation centers must have enclosures large enough for wild birds to learn or re-learn to fly.

FIVE

In the Field

Concerned citizens often deliver distressed wildlife to wildlife rehabilitation centers. But in the case of a large aggressive animal or severely injured one, rehabilitators go out and rescue the animal themselves. When it is time to set the animal free, rehabilitators return to the original site and attempt to release the animal within 3 miles (5 km) of its original home.

Soft Release

Rescuing orphaned wildlife is a rehabilitator's most challenging work. "The babies are the hardest," says Anne, a rehabilitator from Texas. "They come in cold and stressed. We put them in incubators and give them oxygen. When they can eat, we have to mix each one a special baby food and someone feeds the babies every two hours. It's exhausting." Shona Aitken says that the babies are cute and fragile and workers must resist cuddling them. "It just can't be 'hug the bunny,'" she says. "A baby rabbit can actually die from the stress of being near humans. You really have to sneak around and avoid

(Opposite) Once completely healed, most animals recovering in rehabilitation centers will be released back to the wild.

To learn how to survive in the wild, bear cubs are released near dens where wild bear cubs live.
(Opposite) These orphaned deer are being fed by a caregiver at the Wild Forever Rehab Center.

contact." Because baby animals **imprint** on others of their species, usually at 2–5 weeks, rehabilitators have to watch that the babies do not imprint on them. Rehabilitators are silent when they work with the babies. They wear masks and limit how often they handle them. Mike Pratt says, "If you want to cuddle a baby wild animal, you've picked the wrong job. You want these animals to hate you when they leave. If you're too friendly and you turn them loose, you are doing them no favor."

Orphans have the hardest time returning to the wild because they have spent their earliest weeks or months in captivity. In California, Cheryl and Tom Millham operate Lake Tahoe Wildlife Care. Over the years they have rehabilitated dozens of orphaned bear cubs. The Milhams do a "soft release" for their orphaned cubs, meaning that after the cubs are released near a den where wild bear cubs also live, they are monitored by cameras mounted on trees. Rehabilitators use other soft release methods such as leaving food out for the newly released animal to "find" or hanging a small animal in a cage near its eventual release site to get it used to the habitat. "We can raise them healthy, but certain lessons we can't teach them—we can only help them to teach themselves," says rehabilitator Lisa Horn.

Oil Spills

Oil spills are unpredictable and can affect huge populations of wild birds, waterfowl, shorebirds, marine mammals, and sea turtles. These man-made disasters can be daunting to overcome for even the most seasoned rehabilitators.

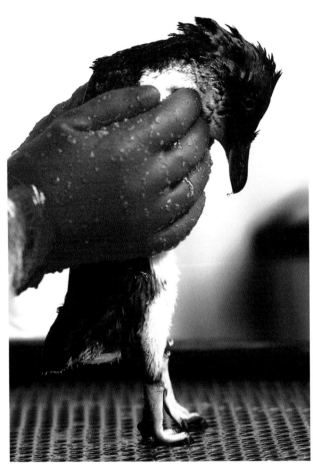

Specially licensed oiled bird rehabilitators come together from all over the world to save animals from oil spills. Here a rescue worker washes an oiled penguin in New Zealand.
(Opposite) This seabird was covered in oil during a massive oil spill in the Gulf of Mexico. It was treated and released at an international bird rescue center in Louisiana.

The worst damage always happens at the beginning of the incident. Sea turtles are a protected species and must be brought to rehabilitation centers immediately. Specially licensed and trained marine rehabilitators care for marine mammals. Rehabilitators licensed for oil spill rescue have a labor-intensive task. After capturing the birds with nets, workers spend about forty-five minutes to clean each one. Once cleaned, the birds are released into wildlife refuges or into clean water near their former location. Birds that need more time to recover are brought back to rehabilitation centers. In large spills, where thousands of birds need care, trained rehabilitators do triage to decide which birds should receive immediate treatment, which will survive but can wait for

Rehabilitation workers have to act fast to save oiled birds.

The birds cannot fly covered in heavy oil nor can they dive for food. They try to clean themselves by picking at their feathers and the oil they ingest poisons them. In 2010, nearly 1,000 wildlife rescue workers worked 6-12 hour shifts, 24 hours a day, cleaning birds damaged by an oil spill in the Gulf of Mexico.

treatment, which will need further rehabilitation in a rehabilitation center, and which should be euthanized quickly. Rehabilitators establish emergency treatment and temporary rehabilitation centers near the spill site and organize volunteers. In the United States, wildlife rescue and rehabilitation workers have saved the lives of hundreds of thousands of animals injured by oil spills.

Eagles in the Field

Mike Pratt tells the story of a tense eagle rescue. A caller spotted a young bald eagle stumbling around a farmer's field. A home-based rehabilitator went to the field, and wearing her heavy leather falconer's gloves, caught the eagle. It was sick, but none of her tests could explain the cause. Later that night two more eagles were found sick in the same field. Caring for three very sick eagles was more than she could handle, so she called Mike to ask for help. It was a two-hour drive and it was late. Mike told the rehabilitator to treat for shock and that someone would come the next day to help. By morning, three more teenage eagles and one adult male were found in the field, also confused and stumbling. Two of the eagles were near death and the cause was still a mystery. Mike thought an **epidemic** might be developing so he contacted the state Fish and Wildlife agency. Wildlife agents did a fly-over of the area and discovered two horse **carcasses** in the back of the field. When they questioned the farmer who owned the land, he explained that he had euthanized his horses, but that his tractor had broken down and he had been unable to dig a hole to bury the corpses. The eagles had been eating horse carcasses saturated with the lethal chemicals used to kill livestock. At the wildlife shelter, the rehabilitators worked around the clock for a week. All seven eagles remarkably survived and were released. Because Mike and his coworkers acted quickly, no other animals, wild or domestic, were poisoned.

One role of a rehabilitator is to monitor the nests and dens of the animals in the area. Knowing where animals live helps rehabilitators release them close to their homes. Here, a rehabilitator is preparing to release a bald eagle into its home territory.

SIX

Into the Wild, Into the Future

Wildlife is a natural resource belonging to the public. State and federal regulations govern the treatment of wild animals. It is illegal in most instances for an unlicensed person to take and keep a wild animal, unless specifically given permission to do so. Wildlife rehabilitators are responsible for being familiar with the latest laws and professional operating standards.

Where Worlds Collide

Most wildlife rehabilitation facilities are located where human population centers and wildlife habitats intersect. In most encounters between humans and wildlife, wildlife suffers. Ninety-eight percent of wild animals brought to rehabilitation centers are victims of human activity, such as habitat loss, pollution, and car accidents. Rehabilitators give the animals a second chance to live in their natural environment.

The Wild Again Wildlife Rehabilitation of Colorado describes wildlife rehabilitation as part science, part education, part problem solving, and part caregiving. Many rehabilitators find themselves in the role of educator. They visit schools, community centers, marinas, sports clubs, and public events to explain how pollution and careless development destroy wild habitats.

(Opposite) Migratory birds travel between Central America and Canada twice each year. U.S. federal and international laws protect them.

Some rehabilitators specialize in conflict resolution. They teach people strategies for coexisting with wild animals and preventing confrontations. Other rehabilitators monitor wildlife for government agencies. Mike Pratt monitored birds in New England. One year he came across an unusual number of dead songbirds. He figured that it was likely a new outbreak of West Nile virus and was able to notify health authorities before the disease spread out of control. In another incident, he noticed an abnormal amount of dead ducks. He called state wildlife agents, who uncovered an illegal toxic waste dumping site.

Grit and Determination

Being a rehabilitator takes more than having a passion for animals. It also takes inner strength and determination to face the job's many challenges and frustrations. Rehabilitators often have to interact with people who have carelessly injured an animal or destroyed its habitat. Many rehabilitators spend countless hours consumed with **fund-raising** instead of caring for animals. Budgets are always tight and rehabilitators frequently engage in fund-raising to pay for basic necessities and, sometimes, their own salaries. Work schedules can be irregular. In a crisis, rehabilitators are called upon to work overtime or to be on call and ready to work if extra help is needed. Many normal schedules involve working night shifts and weekends. Probably the biggest challenge is handling emotional situations. Rehabilitators say it is heartbreaking to work hard to save an animal, only to see it die, or to have to euthanize it. The work can be upsetting even when the rehabilitating is successful and the animal is set free. As Mike Pratt explains, "It's hard to watch them go, but you know you did it right when they run away and look over their shoulder and growl at you!"

Pollution and the destruction of habitat cause countless injuries and unnatural deaths to wildlife each year.

Federal laws that regulate wildlife:

- The Migratory Bird Treaty Act
- The Endangered Species Act
- The Eagle Protection Act
- The Wild Bird Conservation Act
- The National Wildlife Refuge System Administration Act
- The Marine Mammal Protection Act
- The Wild Free-Roaming Horses and Burros Act
- The National Marine Sanctuaries Act

Owls are often injured in nighttime car accidents as they hunt in the dark, frequently near roadways.

Rehabilitators must obtain a special permit from the U.S. Fish and Wildlife Service in order to rescue and treat migratory birds, such as these sandhill cranes.

One of the most important jobs of a rehabilitator is to teach people how to live alongside wildlife. Being particularly cautious while driving in rural areas is key to preventing injuries.

Career Outlook

As humans continue to make inroads to wild areas, habitats are compromised and wild animals are threatened. As development continues, the need for professional wildlife rehabilitators expands. The Bureau of Labor Statistics expects jobs in the field to increase 20 to 25 percent from 2010 to 2020. Rehabilitation centers are nonprofit organizations. They operate on tight budgets and rely on grants and public donations. The average salary range for wildlife rehabilitators employed by a rehabilitation center is $25,000–$35,000 per year. Specialists and educators generally have a higher salary range. Directors are paid more, from $50,000 to $90,000 per year.

While most wildlife rehabilitation workers are employed by private nonprofit rehabilitation centers, some are hired by government agencies to work in wildlife refuges or on oil spill response teams. Their pay range starts at $17 to $25 per hour. Wildlife rescue and rehabilitation is not a high-paying profession. Education costs, however, can be less than other professions and more importantly, job satisfaction is extremely high. Shona Aitken says, "It's what makes me feel good inside. I am not going to get rich, but I love my job!" The director of West Sound Wildlife Shelter in Washington State echoes her thoughts: "Rehabilitation is not for everyone, but these wild animals will catch your heart."

Glossary

associate of science   a two-year degree in the sciences earned at a two- or four-year accredited college or university

bachelor of science   a four-year degree in the sciences earned at an accredited college or university

captivity   the state or period of being confined

carcass   the body of a dead animal

conservation   the act of preserving natural environments

domesticate   to tame an animal to live with and/or provide benefit to humans

enclosure   an area surrounded by a fence, wall, or other type of boundary

endangered species   a species at risk of extinction (no longer existing)

epidemic   an outbreak of a contagious disease that spreads rapidly and widely

euthanize   to humanely put an animal to death to relieve its suffering

first responders   first people to arrive at the scene of an accident or disaster, such as firefighters, emergency medical personnel, or police

fund-raising   an organized activity for collecting money

imprint	a process by which a newborn or very young animal identifies with a parent or parent substitute to learn behavior patterns
incubator	a medical device that closely surrounds a patient to control temperature
natural history	the study and description of living things, their behavior, and how they relate to one another
neurological	having to do with the nervous system
nonprofit	an organization devoted to charitable or educational purposes, where all income is put back into the organization after expenses are paid
ornithology	study of birds
physiology	the study of how organs and systems in the body function
triage	the process of determining the priority of patients' treatments based on the severity of their condition
undergraduate	a college student who has not yet received a bachelor of science or bachelor of arts degree
vital signs	the pulse rate, respiratory rate, body temperature, and blood pressure of a person or animal
waterfowl	a bird that frequently swims in water
wildlife refuge *or* **sanctuary**	a protective location for wildlife in captivity

Find Out More

Books

Field, Shelly. *Career Opportunities in Working with Animals.*
New York: Checkmark Books, 2011.

Hentz, Peggy Sue. *Rescuing Wildlife: A Guide to Helping Injured and Orphaned Animals.* Mechanicsburg, PA: Stackpole Books, 2009.

Lee, Mary Price. *Opportunities in Animal and Pet Care Careers.*
New York: McGraw-Hill, 2009.

Websites

International Wildlife Rehabilitators Council

www.theiwrc.org/

This international organization provides scientific education, publications, classes, and other resources to wildlife rehabilitators. It also provides public information about wildlife conservation and welfare.

National Wildlife Rehabilitator's Association (NWRA)

www.nwrawildlife.org

The National Wildlife Rehabilitator's Association (NWRA) provides information, publications, and classes for wildlife rehabilitators. Wildlife rehabilitators can use the website to exchange ideas, do a job search, and apply for scholarships and grants.

Wildlife Rehabilitation Information Directory

www.wildliferehabinfo.org

This website provides a directory of wildlife rehabilitators in the United States and Canada. The website offers professional rehabilitators and the public information about laws, animal diseases, strategies for coexisting with wildlife, and conflict resolution suggestions.

Index

Page numbers in **boldface** are illustrations.

About the Author

Ruth Bjorklund has written more than 30 nonfiction books for children and young adults. A former children's librarian and craft gallery owner in Seattle, she is interested in art, music, travel, and reading. Her books have covered a wide range of topics from medicine and health, to science, geography, biography, and crafts. She has written several books about animals including endangered wolves, rabbits as pets, komodo dragons, and wild parrots. To do research for this book, Bjorklund visited wildlife centers and met dedicated animal caregivers who were truly amazing. She hopes this book will inform and inspire readers who are considering a career working with wildlife. Ruth Bjorklund lives on an island near Seattle, Washington, where she enjoys watching Great Blue herons and bald eagles soar overhead.